ZOOS
Back to the Wild?

By Bob Barton

Series Literacy Consultant
Dr Ros Fisher

PEARSON
Longman

Pearson Education Limited
Edinburgh Gate
Harlow
Essex CM20 2JE
England

www.longman.co.uk

The rights of Bob Barton to be identified as the authors of this Work have been asserted by him in accordance with the Copyright, Designs and Patents Act, 1988.

Text Copyright © 2004 Pearson Education Limited. Compilation Copyright © 2004 Dorling Kindersley Ltd. All rights reserved. No part of this publication may be reproduced, stored in a retrieval system or transmitted in any form or by any means electronic, mechanical, photocopying, recording, or otherwise, without either the prior written permission of the publishers and copyright owners or a licence permitting restricted copying in the United Kingdom issued by the Copyright Licensing Agency Ltd., 90 Tottenham Court Road, London W1P 9HE

ISBN 0 582 84152 6

Colour reproduction by Colourscan, Singapore
Printed and bound in China by Leo Paper Products Ltd.

The Publisher's policy is to use paper manufactured from sustainable forests.

10 9 8 7 6 5 4 3

DK

The following people from **DK** have contributed to the development of this product:

Art Director Rachael Foster

Martin Wilson **Managing Art Editor** | **Managing Editor** Marie Greenwood
Peter Radcliffe **Design** | **Editorial** Steve Setford, Selina Wood
Marie Ortu **Picture Research** | **Production** Gordana Simakovic
Richard Czapnik, Andy Smith **Cover Design** | **DTP** David McDonald
Consultant David Burnie

Dorling Kindersley would like to thank: Rose Horridge in the DK Picture Library; Penny Smith for editorial assistance; Johnny Pau for additional cover design work.

Picture credits: Heather Angel/Natural Visions: 11tr, 11b, 23; Ardea London Ltd: Francois Gohier 4, 14t, John Daniels 12, Kenneth W. Fink 15; Chester Zoo: 17b; Corbis: Bob Krist 6, 32, David Lees 7tr, Historical Picture Archive 7b, Hulton-Deutsch 8, James L. Amos 26t, Kevin Fleming 25, Paul A. Souders 19; Elk Photography: 9; Robert Harding Picture Library: Robert Francis 13; FLPA - Images of Nature: Terry Whittaker 20, Winifried Wisniewski 22; Melbourne Zoo: Michael Silver/Photonet 14b; Milwaukee County Zoo: Michael Nepper 24; Newspix Archive/Nationwide News: 17tr, 21; N.H.P.A.: E.A. Janes 1c; Outsight Environmental Photography, Thomas Hallstein: 27br; Getty Images: Jim Cummins 29; Photodisc: Russell Illig 26b; Taronga Zoo: 25b; Lake County (IL) Discovery Museum, Curt Teich Postcard Archives: 5; Art Directors & TRIP: 18; Victoria's Open Range Zoo: 3; Roger Williams Park Zoo: 16; Zoological Society of San Diego: 10.
Jacket: Corbis: (front bl), /Mark A. Johnson (front t); FLPA - Images of Nature: Terry Whittaker (back).

All other images: DK Dorling Kindersley © 2004. For further information see www.dkimages.com
Dorling Kindersley Ltd., 80 Strand, London WC2R ORL

Contents

Sunshine or Steel? 4

Open Spaces Are Best 7

Design Is Everything 13

Animals Need Activity 20

We Can Help! 25

Glossary 30

Index 32

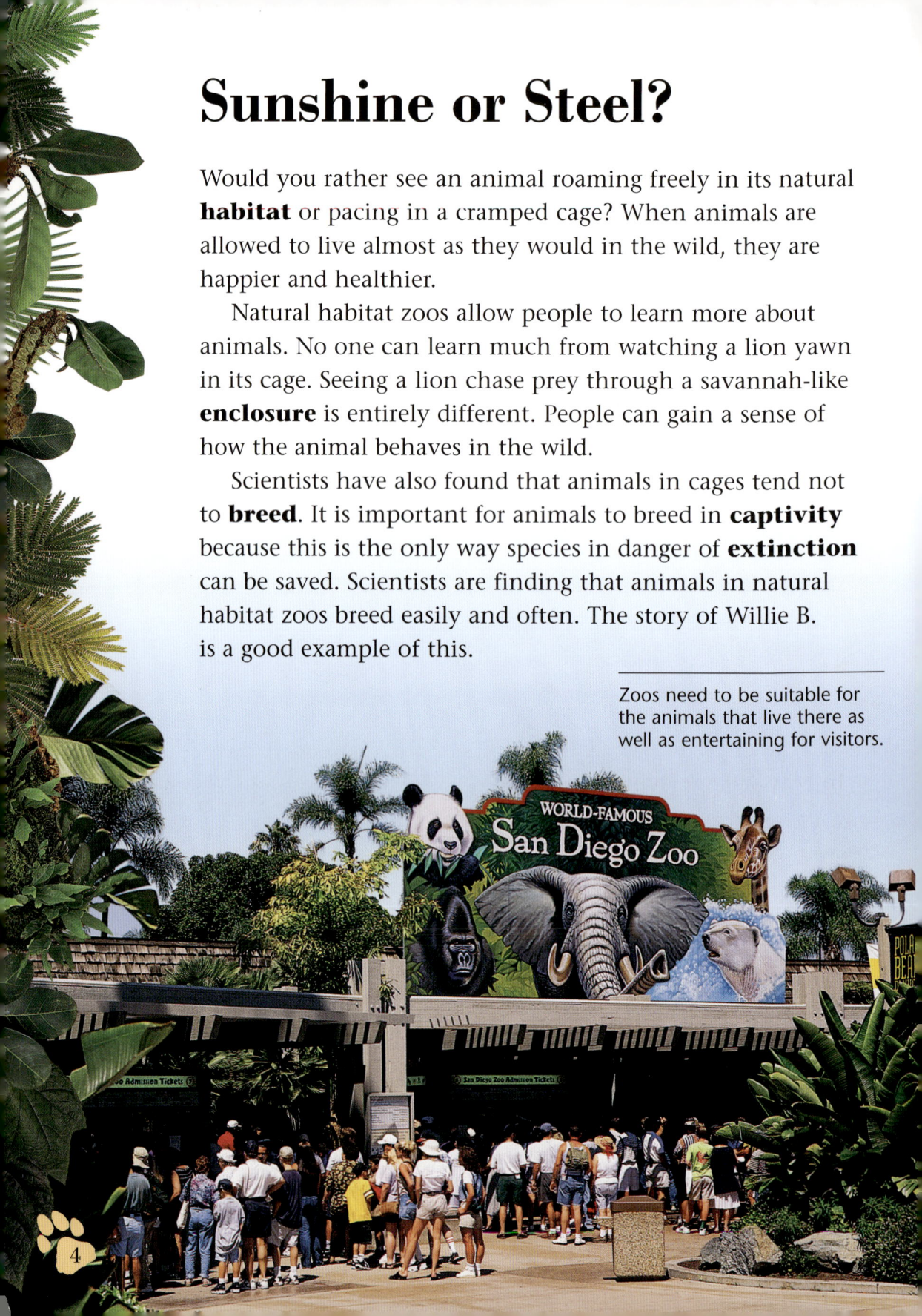

Sunshine or Steel?

Would you rather see an animal roaming freely in its natural **habitat** or pacing in a cramped cage? When animals are allowed to live almost as they would in the wild, they are happier and healthier.

Natural habitat zoos allow people to learn more about animals. No one can learn much from watching a lion yawn in its cage. Seeing a lion chase prey through a savannah-like **enclosure** is entirely different. People can gain a sense of how the animal behaves in the wild.

Scientists have also found that animals in cages tend not to **breed**. It is important for animals to breed in **captivity** because this is the only way species in danger of **extinction** can be saved. Scientists are finding that animals in natural habitat zoos breed easily and often. The story of Willie B. is a good example of this.

Zoos need to be suitable for the animals that live there as well as entertaining for visitors.

In May 1988 television cameras followed Willie B, a western lowland gorilla, as he cautiously entered his new home at Zoo Atlanta, in Atlanta, Georgia, United States. It was designed to resemble Willie B's natural habitat in the Cameroon rainforest. It had a sloping, grassy hillside with thousands of plants and shrubs.

This was the first time Willie B had touched a tree since arriving at Zoo Atlanta in 1961. Willie B had spent his first twenty-seven years at the zoo alone in a concrete cage behind metal bars with only a tyre swing and a television for entertainment. He was overweight from lack of exercise. Willie B often lay on his side and stared into space.

For twenty-seven years, Willie B spent every day in a tiled concrete room. With little to do, he soon became bored and unhealthy.

Fortunately, zoo officials and **vets** had decided to improve Zoo Atlanta. "When I took over the zoo," Terry Maple, the director at Zoo Atlanta, has said, "it was rated as one of the ten worst zoos in America." Today, the zoo is one of the best in the United States.

Willie B spent his last twelve years **socializing** with other gorillas, **foraging** for food and climbing trees. He even became a father. Willie B died peacefully in his sleep in February 2000, but his offspring continue to live happily in Zoo Atlanta.

Here you can see Willie B in his new enclosure. More than 7,000 people came to pay their respects when he died in February 2000.

Open Spaces Are Best

For thousands of years, animals were valued as symbols of power and wealth. The needs of the animals as living creatures, however, were often ignored.

For example, in 1254, the King of England received an elephant from France. He built a stall for the elephant, but there was no room for it to move around. In later centuries, people collected many exotic animals from Africa and Asia and kept them in small wire cages. No one knew how to take care of the animals, so they often suffered.

Romans captured animals and used them for entertainment.

The Royal Menagerie in London in 1816.

Early Zoos

By the 1500s, there was a new interest in natural science.

Carl Hagenbeck replaced the cages in his zoo with natural-looking enclosures.

This interest led to the creation of more zoos in Europe. Usually zoo animals were housed in cages so scientists could watch the animals closely. They were not free to roam, **forage** or **breed**, so little was learned about the animals' natural diets, social lives and movements.

A New Kind of Zoo

In 1907 a man called Carl Hagenbeck opened a zoo in Hamburg, Germany. Hagenbeck had once trained circus animals and knew that caged animals often behaved violently or strangely. In Hagenbeck's zoo, steel bars and wire cages were replaced with more natural-looking **enclosures** surrounded by deep, well-hidden ditches, or **moats**. Hagenbeck knew this would be better for the animals. He hoped it would be better for the visitors, too.

Hagenbeck's zoo was an instant success. Once people had experienced seeing animals in **natural habitats**, they were less interested in seeing animals in zoo enclosures. Soon other zoos sent people to study his design. Many more zoos began to follow Hagenbeck's ideas to consider the animals' welfare as well as the visitors' entertainment and education.

As zoos began to focus on caring for animals in more natural environments, scientific knowledge grew. A new idea also emerged. In addition to educating people, it was thought natural habitat zoos could be used as a way to help save certain species from **extinction**.

In the Living Desert Museum in Palm Springs, Florida, United States, wolves can roam freely in a large, natural enclosure.

Many animal species are facing **extinction** as **natural habitats** rapidly disappear. The logging of rainforests, overfishing, overhunting and water and air pollution threaten the existence of many animal species. As these areas disappear, so do many animal species. Recreating natural habitats in zoos and relocating animals into these environments is one strategy for saving some species while people look for ways to reduce habitat loss in the wild.

Zoos Can Protect Animals

Helping **endangered** species **reproduce** successfully in zoos will also save them from extinction. Births in zoos have increased the populations of Père David's deer, the European bison, the Arabian oryx and the Hawaiian goose. Without these births, these species would have died out.

This calf at the San Diego Zoo in California, United States, is an Arabian oryx, a species once extinct in the wild.

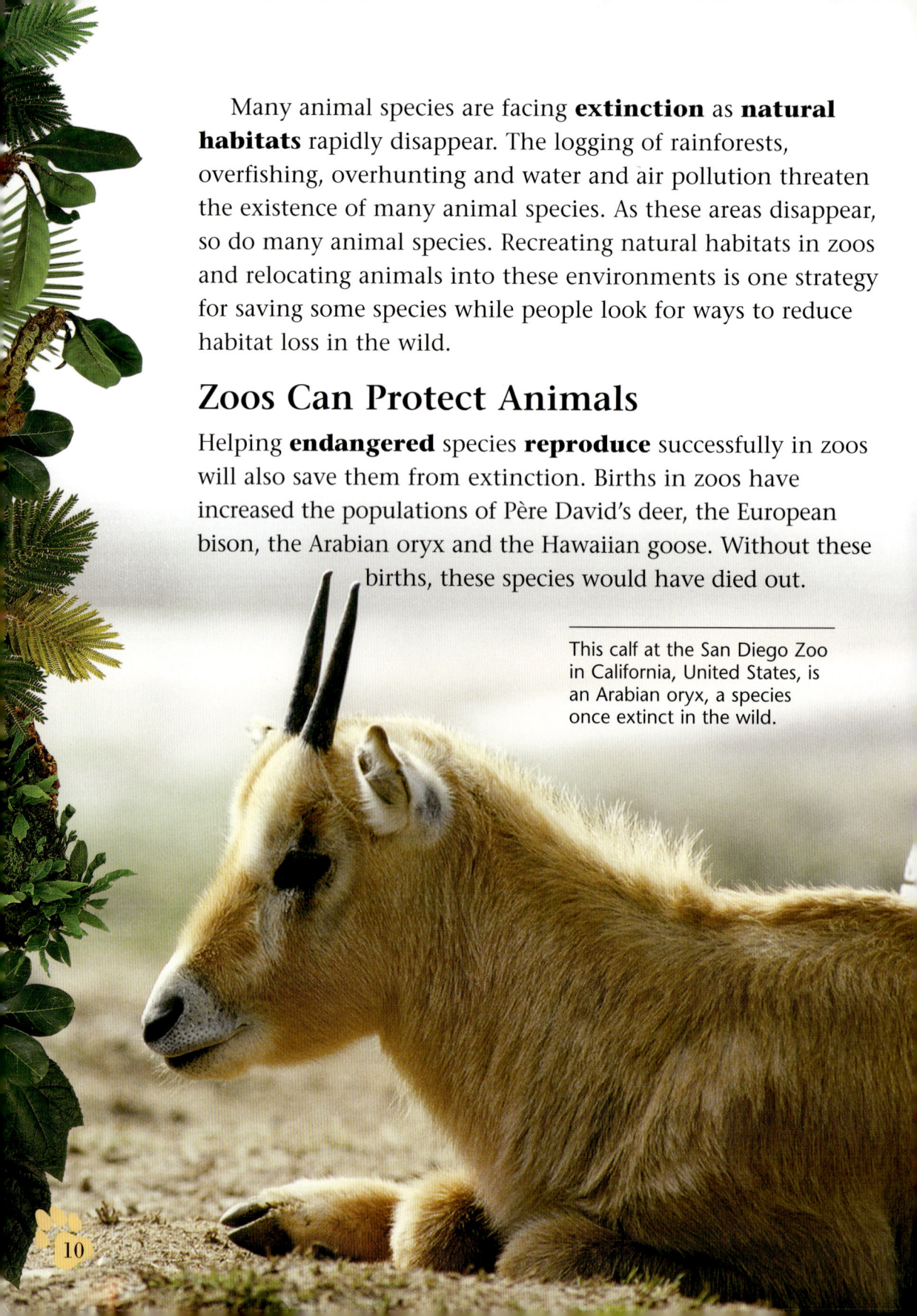

Today, many zoos work to restock protected wild habitats with species that once lived there. First the species **reproduce** in zoos. Then they are released back into their natural environment. For example, the Greater Vancouver Zoo in Canada breeds Oregon spotted frogs and releases them into suitable wetlands. The Toronto Zoo has also returned some species to the wild, including black-footed ferrets, wood bison and Puerto Rican crested toads.

Breeding animals in captivity means fewer animals will be obtained from the wild. The majority of the animals in the Toronto Zoo, for example, do not come from the wild.

Père David's deer are extinct in the wild and can only be seen in zoos and parks. This herd lives in a park in Beijing, China.

Many pandas are born each year at the Giant Panda Breeding Centre in Wolong, Sichuan Province, China.

These vets at the London Zoo are examining a tapir.

Research now shows that animals living in **natural habitat** zoos tend to be healthier and live longer than those in the wild. That's because zoos are a safer, more controlled environment. Zoo vets also study healthy and sick animals to develop better drugs, surgical techniques and medical equipment. In addition, animals receive frequent check-ups and **vaccinations** to keep them healthy.

Education is another important function of modern zoos. In addition to presenting animals in natural habitats, zoos provide informational signs, interactive tours and multimedia displays. These tools teach visitors about each animal's natural behaviour, its role in the environment and the need to conserve natural wildlife habitats. Many visitors leave the zoo with a deeper understanding and respect for animals and the natural world.

Living Longer

Safe from the dangers of life in the wild, polar bears can live up to 25 per cent longer in captivity. The oldest recorded captive bear lived in the Detroit Zoo, in Michigan, United States. It died in 1989 at the age of 42. In their natural habitat, polar bears rarely survive beyond the age of 30.

Design Is Everything

Designing better natural habitats is an ongoing challenge for modern zoos. As **zoologists** and zoo vets learn more about animals, how they interact with their environments and each other, designs for zoo habitats are improved. At the same time, more and more people are visiting zoos. So, it's important that the habitats allow visitors to view the animals safely and clearly.

Successful design elements can be seen in many modern zoos around the world. For example, one feature of an appropriate natural habitat is a **non-intrusive** barrier that protects both the animals and the viewers. Also, visitor-viewing stations are set up in ways that do not disturb the animals. Animal grouping is another consideration. Many animals can be safely grouped with some of the same species that they would live with in the wild. The habitats have **climate** controls to keep them healthy and comfortable.

In this **enclosure**, a colony of prairie dogs live together in surroundings that resemble their natural grassland habitat. A tunnel leads visitors to transparent viewing domes in the centre of the enclosure.

Barriers prevent people from getting too close to the animals and ensure that the animals don't escape. Some common barriers include moats, thick glass and fabricated rocks.

Moats allow the animals to roam while allowing visitors a clear view of the animals' activities.

Moats are often used because they are safe and easy to see across. Dry moats and ditches are effective with large animals, such as elephants, that can't jump very high or far. Water-filled moats are effective for animals that don't like water, such as lions and apes. Specially strengthened glass or nets of thin wire contain animals that can leap or fly over other barriers. Behind these barriers, animals have space to move about freely.

The glass walls and roof of the Butterfly House at the Melbourne Zoo, Australia, allow the butterflies inside to fly freely but also prevent them from escaping.

Open Range Zoos Provide Space

Some zoos have taken further steps to remove barriers between the animals and the visitors. Open range zoos are huge parks that offer animals more space to roam. In an ordinary zoo, visitors view animals up close. In an open range zoo, visitors view the animals at a distance from a train or a coach.

At the 850-hectare San Diego Wild Animal Park in California, United States, visitors can take a train past herds of antelopes, giraffes, deer, zebras, rhinoceroses and other animals. While the animals roam freely, the movements of the people are controlled. Parks such as this one give animals more freedom to behave naturally and raise their young, while visitors enjoy a more natural zoo experience.

The conditions in open range zoos make it easier for animals to **breed** and care for their young. This is the East African section of the San Diego Wild Animal Park.

Viewing Areas Protect

Zoos can improve habitats by providing viewing areas that don't interfere with the animals' normal activities. Many zoos provide underwater viewing stations for people to see animals such as polar bears and sea lions. These viewing stations allow the animals to behave naturally but still give visitors a chance to watch them.

Special viewing areas were built at the gorilla exhibition at Zoo Atlanta. These observation platforms are above the habitat. They provide visitors with excellent views of the apes **foraging** for food, challenging each other or caring for their babies. They also keep the visitors far enough away not to distract or disturb the gorillas.

Polar bears enjoy swimming underwater, which normally hides them from zoo visitors. **Exhibitions** like this one allow visitors to view the bears without disturbing them.

Animal Grouping Is Natural

Today, zoos are often grouping animals according to their natural geographical environments. These environments include deserts, grasslands and mountain highlands. Animals benefit because these environments are more diverse and more suitable in terms of natural materials. They also give visitors a better sense of the animals' natural habitat.

The 1-hectare gelada baboon exhibition at the Bronx Zoo in New York is one example of this type of habitat. The baboons in the exhibition live peacefully side by side with Nubian ibex and rock hyrax. The space is planned so that the animals have choices for **socializing** and foraging, much as they would in the African highlands. The Emmen Zoo in the Netherlands groups more than ten species together in its African savannah habitat including rhinos, zebras, giraffes, impalas and gnus.

Zebras and giraffes live side by side in the Savannah Exhibition at the Melbourne Zoo, Australia, just as they do in the wild, on Africa's grassy plains.

Modern zoos keep animals in enclosures similar to their homes in the wild, as in the chimpanzee colony at Chester Zoo.

Climate Control

The Biodome in Montreal, Canada, turned a former Olympic stadium into four different **ecosystems** including two different kinds of forests, a marine environment and a polar habitat. The tropical forest, for example, houses many different species of plants, birds, reptiles and mammals in a temperature- and humidity-controlled indoor environment. Visitors walk along a path that takes them past high trees, plants, a waterfall, a cave, a river and rugged cliffs. The realistic rocks, trees and cave are all made of concrete. A fine mist comes from the trees to water the plants and to make the environment feel tropical.

By simulating hot deserts, freezing polar regions or tropical rain forests, zoos provide the types of environments that animals need to stay healthy. These exhibitions also teach visitors about animals' habitats.

Lions, such as this one in the Asheboro Zoo, in North Carolina, United States, like hot weather. The rocks in their enclosure may be fitted with heating coils.

Nocturnal Animals

Some animals are **nocturnal**. Zoos reverse day and night so visitors can learn more about them. The **marsupial exhibition** at Australia's Taronga Zoo is one such place. During the day, a dim, moonlike light simulates night-time for the animals.

In other zoos, daylight is reversed by shining red fluorescent light on the animals during the day and white light for the rest of the time. The red light is invisible to the animals, so they wake up when it comes on. When the white light shines, they go to sleep.

All over the world, zookeepers are working hard to create safe natural habitats for animals. The natural habitat zoos protect endangered species and give them a better opportunity to reproduce. They also teach visitors important lessons about **conservation** and respect for wildlife.

The Taronga Zoo in Sydney, Australia, has a marsupial exhibition that gives visitors a unique view of the activities of nocturnal animals, like the koala.

Animals Need Activity

Natural habitats have greatly improved the lives of animals kept in zoos. A natural environment is only part of the picture, though. Zookeepers also search for new ways to keep animals in **captivity** active and alert. This is called **enrichment**.

In the wild, animals hunt for food, avoid predators, care for their young and **socialize**. In zoos, however, zookeepers feed the animals and keep them safe from predators. Without activities or other stimulation, zoo animals often sleep too much, eat too much, gain weight and refuse to **breed**. Giving these animals problems to solve or a choice of actions enriches and helps lengthen their lives.

Toys like logs, tyres and boulders help keep bears in zoos from becoming bored.

This elephant at the Taronga Zoo, Australia, is enjoying playing with a bungee ball.

Finding the Right Enrichment

It is important for zookeepers to provide the correct type of enrichment for each animal. For example, in the wild, a fennec fox digs in mounds of sand, so digging is important for its enrichment. Elephants and chimpanzees are highly intelligent and social, so their activities often involve games and socializing. Elephants like playing with large balls. Chimps compete with one another by swinging in trees.

Some zoos find surprising ways to enrich the lives of their animals. In the wild, elephants use their trunks to scratch in the dirt with sticks or rocks. Ruby, an Asian elephant at the Phoenix Zoo in Arizona, United States, did her scratching with paintbrushes. She painted pictures on an easel. Her keeper handed her the brushes and she applied the strokes. Of course, not all elephants want to paint. Finding the right enrichment is up to the zookeeper.

Bears must solve problems to find food in the wild, such as how to catch fish in fast-flowing rivers.

Finding food in the wild takes up much of an animal's time, so zookeepers try to replicate this time in enrichment activities. Chimpanzees at the Lowry Park Zoo in Tampa, Florida, United States, use twigs to scoop honey and jam out of an artificial termite mound. In the wild, this is how they would gather termites.

The bear **exhibition** at the Woodland Park Zoo in Seattle, Washington, United States, has a vast area strewn with logs, trees and boulders for the bears to play with. There is also a stream stocked with trout, which helps recreate the bears' natural environment and encourages them to **forage** for food.

Effective enrichment can be simple. At London Zoo a female kinkajou, a South American member of the raccoon family, spent most of her time chasing her own tail. Zookeepers hung apples from strings above the kinkajou. To get them, she had to climb up and use her tail. As a result, the tail-chasing stopped.

Animals Need Company

Some animals need to **socialize** with others of their kind. In the wild, hippopotamuses live in herds of five to thirty animals. The Emmen Zoo in the Netherlands has a herd of nine hippos, the largest of any European zoo. Hippos are social animals and this type of environment provides them with a better chance for normal **reproduction** and healthy lives.

By keeping a herd of Asian water buffalo, Port Lympne Zoo in Kent allows the buffalo to socialize with each other.

In the wild, cheetahs would eat antelopes. At the Milwaukee County Zoo in Wisconsin, United States, they live side by side, separated by a deep moat.

Finding meaningful, safe enrichment activities for animals living in **captivity** is an ongoing challenge. Whether it's providing polar bears with giant rubber balls to play with, placing crickets in an **enclosure** for fennec foxes to stalk and eat, or providing mud wallows and dust baths for the elephants to lounge in, interesting new options are always being explored. No animal should be left alone to become bored in front of a television, as the gorilla Willie B. once was. Zookeepers know that enriching animals' lives is important. The animals stay healthier and happier, and visitors see animals behaving as they do in the wild.

We Can Help!

Wildlife is an essential part of the world's **ecosystem**. That is why the survival of threatened species is important. Zoos work hard to protect these species, and they need your help. Here are some suggestions for how you can support **natural habitat** zoos and help promote the well-being and survival of Earth's wildlife.

These children are examining a donkey at their local zoo.

Zoos teach visitors about preserving natural habitats and protecting wildlife. A zoo worker at the Taronga Zoo in Sydney, Australia, is helping this girl to learn about koalas.

What You Can Do

- Check with a zoo in your area to see if it offers classes about specific animals and their habitats. Some zoos offer tours that let you watch trainers work with, feed and care for animals.

- Talk to the zookeepers on your next visit to the zoo. Many zoos have volunteers who answer questions about animals and their habitats.

People who work at the zoo can answer questions and give you more information about the animals.

A zoo tour can help you to appreciate the animals much more. Supervised by a zookeeper, you may be able to handle some of the animals.

Conservation Fund

In 2000 the Auckland Zoo in New Zealand started the Conservation Fund to help projects that are working to conserve natural habitats in the wild. One project is trying to restore kiwis and other birds to the Waipoua Forest in New Zealand. Another project hopes to save endangered turtles in North Vietnam. Money for the fund comes from programmes at the zoo and from other donations.

Kiwis are flightless birds that live in New Zealand's woodlands.

- Volunteer to help at a local children's zoo. Some zoos offer opportunities for people to spend a few hours a week assisting zookeepers in caring for the animals.

- Help save an endangered species by learning all you can about it. Let others know what you find out. Many scientists have published important facts about animals living in the wild. Jane Goodall's work with wild chimpanzees, for example, helped zookeepers find meaningful enrichment activities for the chimps in their care.

Working alongside a zookeeper helps children better understand the animals and their needs.

27

Make a Zoo Checklist

A zoo checklist can include things to look for and questions to ask the zookeepers. Here are a few ideas for you:

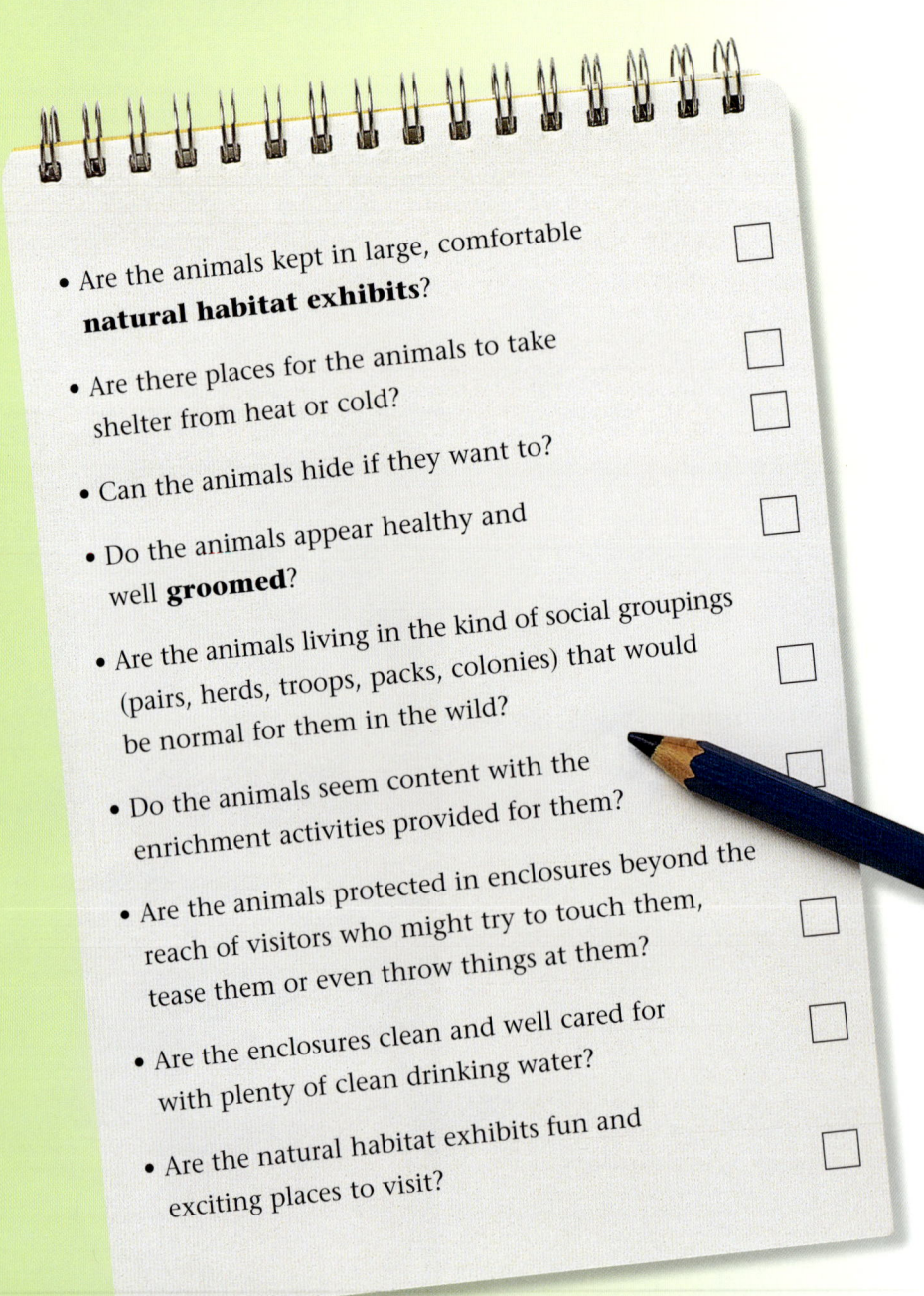

- Are the animals kept in large, comfortable **natural habitat exhibits**? ☐
- Are there places for the animals to take shelter from heat or cold? ☐
- Can the animals hide if they want to? ☐
- Do the animals appear healthy and well **groomed**? ☐
- Are the animals living in the kind of social groupings (pairs, herds, troops, packs, colonies) that would be normal for them in the wild? ☐
- Do the animals seem content with the enrichment activities provided for them? ☐
- Are the animals protected in enclosures beyond the reach of visitors who might try to touch them, tease them or even throw things at them? ☐
- Are the enclosures clean and well cared for with plenty of clean drinking water? ☐
- Are the natural habitat exhibits fun and exciting places to visit? ☐

After Your Visit

After visiting the zoo, look over the notes on the checklist. If you feel you have positive suggestions about making the zoo better, work with your teacher or an adult to share your ideas and concerns. Here are some actions you can take:

Take notes on everything you have learned about zoos. You may wish to illustrate your notes.

- Write a letter to the organization or board of directors that oversees the zoo. You can find this information at the zoo offices, in brochures about the zoo, or on the Internet.

- Write a letter to your local newspaper informing readers about your concerns.

- Support zoos that you feel provide all the things on your checklist. Visit them often and tell others about the zoos you like.

Glossary

breed — the ability of animals to give birth to their young

captivity — being held in one place, often by force

climate — the weather conditions of an environment such as temperature, humidity and rainfall

conservation — the protection of natural things such as animals and plants

ecosystems — the animals, plants and bacteria that make up particular communities living in certain environments

enclosure — a space surrounded by fences or other barriers

endangered — in danger of being destroyed or dying out

enrichment — activities for animals that are like the kinds of things they do in the wild

exhibition — a display

extinction — the dying out of a species

foraging	searching for food
groomed	to have cleaned (esp. an animal's coat)
habitat	the home of an animal or plant in the wild
marsupial	an animal with a pouch
moats	deep, wide ditches used as barriers to enclose animals
natural habitat exhibitions	displays designed to show plants and animals in their normal environments
nocturnal	active at night
non-intrusive	does not interfere with
reproduce	to produce offspring of the same kind
socializing	living together cooperatively
vaccinations	injections that prevent animals from getting certain diseases
vets	animal doctors
zoologists	people who study animals and animal life

Index

Arabian oryx 10
antelope 24
apes 14
Asian water buffalo 23
baboons 17
barriers 13–15
bears 20, 22
Biodome 18
black-footed ferrets 11
buffalo 23
butterflies 14
cheetah 24
chimpanzees 17, 21, 22, 27
climate control 13, 18
crickets 24
deer 15
elephants 7, 14, 21, 24
European bison 10
fennec fox 21, 24
giraffes 15, 17
gnus 17
gorrilas 5–6, 16
grouping animals 13, 17
Hagenbeck, Carl 8–9
Hawaiian goose 10
hippopotamuses 23
impala 17
kinkajou 23
kiwis 27
kuala 19
lions 18
Maple, Terry 6

moats 8, 14, 24
nocturnal animals 19
Nubian ibex 17
open range zoos 15
Oregon spotted frog 11
pandas 11
Père David's deer 11
polar bears 12, 16, 24
prairie dogs 13
Puerto Rican crested toads 11
rhinoceroses 15, 17
rock hyrax 17
Ruby 21
sea lions 16
tapirs 12
turtles 27
vets 6, 12, 13
viewing stations 13, 16
Willie B. 5–6, 24
wolves 9
wood bison 11
zebras 15, 17